How To Use Time-Out

SECOND EDITION

R. Vance Hall
and
Marilyn L. Hall

How To Manage Behavior Series

R. Vance Hall
and
Marilyn L. Hall
Series Editors

pro·ed
An International Publisher
8700 Shoal Creek Boulevard
Austin, Texas 78757-6897
800/897-3202 Fax 800/397-7633
Order online at http://www.proedinc.com

8700 Shoal Creek Boulevard
Austin, Texas 78757-6897
800/897-3202 Fax 800/397-7633
Order online at http://www.proedinc.com

Library of Congress Cataloging-in-Publication Data

Hall, R. Vance (Robert Vance), 1928–
    How to use time out / R. Vance Hall, Marilyn L. Hall.—2nd ed.
      p.   cm.—(How to manage behavior series)
    Includes bibliographical references.
    ISBN 0-89079-768-4 (alk. paper)
    1. Behavior modification.   2. Timeout method.   I. Hall, Marilyn
  C. II. Title. III. Series
LB1060.2.H358   1998
371.15'3—dc21   97-32522
                                                 CIP

This book is designed in Palatino and Frutiger.

Printed in the United States of America

 6 7 8 9 10 11 12 13 14   13

Contents

Preface to Series

The first edition of the *How To Manage Behavior Series* was launched some 15 years ago in response to a perceived need for teaching aids that could be used by therapists and trainers. The widespread demand for the series has demonstrated the need by therapists and trainers for nontechnical materials for training and treatment aids for parents, teachers, and students. Publication of this revised series includes many updated titles of the original series. In addition, several new titles have been added, largely in response to therapists and trainers who have used the series. A few titles of the original series that proved to be in less demand have been replaced. We hope the new titles will increase the usefulness of the series.

The editors are indebted to Steven Mathews, Vice President of PRO-ED, who was instrumental in the production of the revised series, as was Robert K. Hoyt, Jr. of H & H Enterprises in producing the original version.

These books are designed to teach practitioners, including parents, specific behavioral procedures to use in managing the behaviors of children, students, and other persons whose behavior may be creating disruption or interference at home, at school, or on the job. The books are nontechnical, step-by-step instructional manuals that define the procedure, provide numerous examples, and allow the reader to make oral or written responses.

The exercises in these books are designed to be used under the direction of someone (usually a professional) with a background in the behavioral principles and procedures on which the techniques are based.

The booklets in the series are similar in format but are flexible enough to be adapted to a number of different teaching situations and training environments.

As always, we invite your comments, suggestions, and questions. We are always happy to hear of your successes in changing your own behaviors and the behaviors of other persons to make your lives more pleasant, productive, and purposeful.

R. Vance Hall &
Marilyn L. Hall,
Series Editors

How To Manage Behavior Series

How To Maintain Behavior

How To Motivate Others Through Feedback

How To Negotiate a Behavioral Contract

How To Select Reinforcers

How To Teach Social Skills

How To Teach Through Modeling and Imitation

How To Use Group Contingencies

How To Use Planned Ignoring

How To Use Prompts To Initiate Behavior

How To Use Response Cost

How To Use Systematic Attention and Approval

How To Use Time-Out

Introduction

This manual provides information and exercises for persons who want to learn to use time-out. Time-out is a mild but effective punishment procedure that takes the place of nagging and spanking. By studying this book and carrying out the exercises, parents, teachers, employers, and others can learn to use time-out in a systematic way and with consistently favorable results.

Knowing how to use time-out correctly is especially important to persons who dislike using spanking or other forms of physical punishment, persons who find themselves becoming angry and emotional in dealing with misbehavior, and persons who find nagging and reprimanding to be ineffective. Time-out is an important procedure for persons who feel the children they are responsible for are "out of control."

The exercises in this booklet are best used under the direction of a professional who has a background in the behavioral principles and procedures on which time-out is based. The exercises should be completed by the person going through the program. Feedback and discussion about the exercises should be provided by the professional during two or more sessions. In some cases, effective feedback can be given over the telephone.

Some persons will be able to begin using time-out with very little assistance other than the instruction provided here. Others will need more explanation and coaching, as well as attention and approval for their efforts. Some persons find this to be a very difficult program in the beginning, but if they stick with it, they are the ones who usually profit most from using time-out.

This manual is designed to be used mostly with young children, but examples of time-out with teenagers and in business applications are included to demonstrate how the principles generalize to other settings and other problems. Although most of the definitive research on time-out was carried out in the 1960s and 1970s, there are a number of recent texts available, such as that by Kazdin (1994), that give good reviews of token procedures.

R. Vance Hall, PhD, is Senior Scientist Emeritus of The Bureau of Child Research and Professor Emeritus of Human Development and Family Life and Special Education at the University of Kansas. He was a pioneer in carrying out behavioral research in classrooms and in homes. Marilyn L. Hall, EdD, taught and carried out research in regular and special public school classrooms. While at the University of Kansas, she developed programs for training parents to use systematic behavior change procedures and was a successful behavior therapist specializing in child management and marriage relationships.

What Is Time-Out?

With Young Children

Steve and Debra Good were desperate because their son, Sean, and daughter, Meghann, ages 4 and 6, seemed to constantly be fighting. Worse, the fights seemed to be escalating and their parents were concerned that one or the other might be seriously injured if they continued. Mrs. Good's efforts at discipline during the day (including scolding and spanking) were ineffective. Mr. Good's attempts to reason with Sean and Meghann when he came home in the evening were also of no avail.

They sought professional help and learned how to use a systematic procedure that included having both Sean and Meghann sit on a chair facing a wall for a short time every time they fought. This simple procedure quickly resulted in a sharp decrease of fighting. The result was that Sean and Meghann actually began to enjoy playing together and their parents reported greatly improved family relationships (based on Olson & Roberts, 1987).

At School

Margaret was a 9-year-old enrolled in a class for children with multiple disabilities. In addition to being developmentally delayed, she had limited vision, hearing, and hand and hip deformities. Margaret's teachers and parents were extremely concerned about her frequent and severe temper tantrums. She had become so uncontrollable that she was making very little academic or social progress. Instead of doing her schoolwork or interacting appropriately with her classmates, she threw tantrums. Her tantrums included screaming "No" or "I won't," stamping her foot, and spitting at people. Attempts at ignoring these behaviors had proved unsuccessful because Margaret was so disruptive that it was difficult not to give her attention. Finally the teachers began requiring Margaret to sit on a chair in the hall for 1 minute each time she screamed. Screaming increased for one day and then began to decrease. Then the teachers began the same procedure for foot stamping. After a 1-day increase, stamping too began to decline. Two days after beginning the same procedure for spitting, spitting also stopped. Thus, within 16 days, Margaret's tantrums were eliminated. Thereafter, her academic and social development progressed satisfactorily (Brown, Nesbitt, Purvis, & Cossairt, 1978).

In Business

A safety program was instituted in a large midwest chemical plant. Its main feature was a program that rewarded workers who had no lost-time accidents or injuries. The longer workers went without lost-time injuries, the greater their chances of receiving rewards, which included money, tickets to sporting events, and paid weekend vacations. This program was quite effective and did result in reduced accident rates. However, there were still a few workers who had frequent lost-time injuries. For these workers, a system was instituted to suspend them from the job for a short period if more than two lost-time injuries occurred within a given time. This resulted in a sharp decrease in lost-time accidents among injury-prone workers (E. Ritschl, personal communication, 1979).

These three incidents illustrate the use of time-out to decrease undesirable behavior. Even though humans have been using some form of time-out in everyday life since very early times, only since the 1960s have psychologists carried out research to verify the importance of following certain steps in order to assure that time-out works effectively. Persons who attempt to use time-out without following certain basic rules are likely to fail. Unfortunately, they are then likely to resort to nagging, spanking, or other forms of discipline that may be not only ineffective but actually harmful.

Time-out should be free of ridicule and degradation. The old-time procedure of forcing a child to stand in a corner in a classroom, to wear a dunce cap and sit on a stool, or to stand with his or her nose in a chalk ring on the blackboard could be called time-out, but such procedures also ridicule the child in the eyes of his or her peers and are more likely to cause resentment and anger than positive behavior changes.

Time-out is a form of discipline that, if properly used, is almost always effective in decreasing unwanted behavior. It is an alternative to corporal punishment. Time-out does not expose children to bodily harm and it preserves the dignity and integrity of the adult using it. It is effective with children with well-established oppositional behavior that is "out of control" and that has not responded to systematic attention and approval or planned ignoring procedures.

Defining Time-Out

Having read the introduction to this manual, you probably have a good idea of what is meant by time-out. The full term is time-out from social reinforcement. Time-out is a procedure for decreasing a specific unwanted behavior by removing a person from the opportunity to receive attention and other rewards whenever he or she engages in that specific undesired behavior.

In your own words, describe what time-out is and what it does.

What time-out is: _____

_____

_____

(continues)

What time-out does: _____

_____

_____

You are right if you said time-out is a procedure that removes a person from the opportunity to receive attention and other rewards when he or she engages in a certain behavior.

Describe an event or situation you have observed in which time-out or an attempt at time-out was used.

_____

_____

Was it effective? _____

_____

Describe a situation you have observed in which you think time-out could or should have been used to decrease a behavior.

_____

_____

_____

_____

Now that we have defined and given examples of time-out, it may seem to be a very simple and straightforward procedure. However, time-out is very frequently misused, and if it is misused, it is very likely to be ineffective. It is also sometimes very difficult for persons to begin using time-out unless they know exactly what they are doing, how to introduce it, and how to cope with resistance behaviors they may expect when introducing time-out.

You now know what is meant by time-out and you understand its effects on behavior when it is properly implemented. You are now ready to learn the basic steps for using time-out to decrease an undesirable behavior in someone you know or with whom you work.

Even though you understand the basic principle of using time-out, you should follow through on each step to increase your chances of being successful with time-out on your first attempt.

Basic Steps in Using Time-Out

▶ **Step 1: Select candidates for using time-out.**

What persons are good candidates for time-out? Time-out can be used successfully with a wide range of persons, including adults. In the home it has been used most widely and effectively with children from 2 to 12 years old. In institutions time-out is used with persons of all ages with all kinds of developmental and behavioral problems. In sports and business time-out is used effectively with adults, for example, in the penalty box in hockey and with short employment suspensions for unsafe acts or absenteeism in industry.

Attempts at time-out are probably most often misapplied to teenagers. Parents almost always violate basic time-out procedures when they resort to "grounding." That is one of the reasons parents who frequently resort to grounding are at odds with their teenagers and do not find grounding to be effective in bringing about change. Among the mistakes these parents make are the following:

1. Parents do not pinpoint a behavior and tell the teenager in advance what specific behavior will cause grounding.

2. Parents make grounding last too long. This is especially true when parents ground their teenagers for an entire weekend or even for extreme periods of up to 6 weeks. This makes it difficult to use grounding following each occurrence of the behavior it is designed to decrease. Such a penalty is effective at the most only once during that entire period. This limits its usefulness and often eliminates the opportunity for the teenager to practice the desired behavior. Another error parents make is to administer grounding while angry. As a result, the teenager may feel the punishment was a result of the parents' anger rather than because of the misbehavior.

With teenagers, contingency contracting is usually more effective than time-out. However, brief, contingent time-out from the telephone, stereo, and television can be effective with adolescents.

School principals also frequently misuse time-out when they give teenagers out-of-school suspensions. Suspending a student from school for being absent, for smoking, or for many other behaviors is most likely to put that student in greater contact with the outside reinforcers he or she wants. Confining students (in-school suspension) for short periods to an uninteresting room within the school building is much more effective than out-of-school suspension in decreasing undesired behavior in teenagers.

Time-out may not be appropriate for children with histories of engaging in self-stimulation. Children who spend a good deal of time engaging in "autistic-like" behavior, such as hand flapping, may find time-out reinforcing if it allows them to engage in those behaviors without interruption.

_____

Indicate here the name, age, and relationship (i.e., student, son, client, employee) of the person(s) whose behavior you intend to change using time-out.

Name(s) _____

Age(s) _____

Relationship(s) _____

▶ **Step 2: Define or pinpoint the behavior you want to change.**

The next step is to decide exactly what behavior(s) to change. Because time-out decreases behavior, it is necessary to pinpoint a behavior you do not want. This is usually not too difficult because people tend to notice behaviors that irritate and annoy more than behaviors that are pleasing. In using time-out, it is also important to identify behaviors you want to increase and maintain.

A good definition of the behavior you want to change through time-out will answer the following questions: Who? What? When? and Where?—that is, whose behavior is being pinpointed, what is the behavior, and when and where does it take place?

Holly Park was concerned about her relationship with her 5-year-old daughter, Cristen. She found herself yelling and threatening to spank Cristen for screaming, fighting, disobeying, and bossing at home. Holly was frequently on the verge of tears, and on some occasions she spanked Cristen so hard that afterwards it left Holly feeling upset and guilty. In spite of the yelling, threats, and spankings, Cristen seemed to be increasingly defiant and uncooperative. She often refused to obey her mother when asked to do something. She also frequently took toys away from her 3-year-old brother, pushed, hit, or even kicked him so that he came crying to his mother. Holly also found that she and her husband were frequently at odds about Cristen. He accused her of being either too lenient or too harsh with Cristen, though he himself did not seem to be able to do any better (based on Roberts, Hatzenbueler, & Bean, 1981; Zeilberger, Sampen, & Sloane, 1968).

When asked to define the behavior she wished to change, Holly first said she wanted to stop Cristen's defiance and hostility. With a little guidance she pinpointed defiance as instances when Cristen failed to begin to carry out her direct instructions within 5 seconds, or when she responded to requests by saying, "No," "I won't," or any other negative statement, whether or not she did what she was asked to do. Holly decided to record Cristen's responses to the first 10 instructions she gave from the time Cristen awakened each morning.

It was a good definition because it answered the who, what, when, and where questions. Cristen was who; failure to begin to carry out instructions within 5 seconds or responding negatively to requests was what; the first 10 responses to Holly's requests wherever they occurred were the when and where.

Practicing Pinpointing

In the situation below, pinpoint a behavior that might be a target for time-out.

Ron Van Hout, an attendant in a state institution, is concerned about Louie, a 9-year-old boy who is developmentally delayed and who has no speech and does not respond to commands. Although Ron is convinced that Louie is capable of learning language, Ron has been unable to work with Louie because every time he is taken to a speech therapy room, Louie climbs on his chair or comes around to where Ron is seated. Louie then smiles and attempts to shake Ron's hand. If Ron attempts to ignore Louie, Louie hugs him around the waist, smiles, and makes guttural noises. Ron realizes that these are ways Louie has learned to get attention from attendants and from visitors on the ward, but he also knows that these persistent habits are interfering with his education.

Describe a behavior Ron might pinpoint and change.

Who? _____

_____

_____

(continues)

What? _____

_____

_____

Where? _____

_____

_____

When? _____

_____

_____

Did you focus on a specific behavior Ron might decrease? Yes ☐ No ☐

If you were able to check yes, good!

Did you answer the questions who, what, where, and when? Yes ☐ No ☐

Remember, in defining a behavior, avoid using labels. People sometimes say they are concerned about hostility, negativism, resistance, aggression, or attitudes. If you used such a label in the example above, try instead to focus on a specific behavior. Such labels are usually vague and mean too many different things to different persons.

Describe how you would pinpoint a behavior you would like to change using time-out. (Try to choose a simple but important one with which you think you will have success on your first try. Remember, select only one behavior even though there may be several you would like to change.)

Who? _____

What? _____

Where? _____

When? _____

(continues)

Check your answers with the person who is working with you on this problem. If you both agree that the definition is a good one, make a check here ☐. If not, work on your definition until you can put a check in the box.

▶ **Step 3: Measure the behavior selected.**

Now it is time to get an idea about the level of the behavior you want to change. This is important for two reasons:

1. You may find that the behavior you wish to change is not as much of a problem as you thought. If that happens, so much the better. Then the thing to do is define another behavior to decrease with time-out.

2. Measuring the behavior will help you to see whether time-out really changes the behavior. If you are measuring the ongoing behavior, you will be able to see when it begins to decrease. This will encourage you to continue using time-out until you are successful.

Most behaviors that lend themselves to time-out can be measured by one of the following procedures.

Counting Behavior

There are several ways to measure behavior. One common procedure is to count the behavior each time it happens. Fights, talking back, noncompliance, tantrums, and arguments are easy to keep track of by making a tally with paper and pencil each time the behavior occurs.

One teacher counted the number of times a student left his seat without permission by marking on a piece of masking tape on his wrist. At the end of the period, it was easy to see and record on the calendar how many times the student left his seat. Over a 5-day period, the teacher recorded 7, 6, 4, 5 and 8 incidents, for a total of 30 out of seats, or an average of 6 a day.

Percent of Behavior

Sometimes we are interested in tallying the percentage of occurrence of a behavior. In the case previously mentioned (of Holly and Cristin), Holly kept track of how many times Cristin responded to her requests appropriately out of the first 10 requests she made each day. The percentages were simple to compute: 3 of 10 = 30%, 5 of 10 = 50%, 7 of 10 = 70%. One day Holly asked Cristen to do something only six times and Cristen complied three times (3 of 6 = 50%). Another day Cristen complied on 3 of 9 requests (33%).

Timing Behaviors

In some cases, how long a behavior lasts may be more important to know than how many times it occurs. A parent may get a better idea of how much arguing her children do by recording how long the arguments last rather than how many times they occur. There may be from one to six arguments every evening, but one long argument may last as long as six shorter ones. Such behaviors may be timed by a stopwatch, but keeping track on a wrist-watch or kitchen clock is accurate enough to get a good estimate of how long a behavior lasts.

In the following example, a parent kept a record of how many minutes it took her daughter to do the dishes each night after supper.

Mon	Tue	Wed	Thurs	Fri
7:01– 7:55 = 54	6:35– 7:40 = 65	6:20– 7:40 = 80	6:45– 7:25 = 40	6:50– 8:20 = 90
54 min	65 min	80 min	40 min	90 min

Selecting a Measurement Procedure

Describe how you will measure the level of the behavior you plan to change so you will later be able to determine whether or not time-out is having an effect. (Remember, it is very important to know the level of the behavior before you try to change it.)

_____

_____

_____

_____

_____

If your instructor agrees that the method you have chosen is a good one, put a check here ☐. If there is a question about your measurement procedure, work on it until you can put a check in the box.

Recording the Behavior

Although you may be keeping a record of the behavior on a special piece of paper, a calendar, or somewhere else, also record it in the space below so your instructor can easily check your record:

Day or Session	1	2	3	4	5	6	7	8	9	10
Level of Behavior										

Keep recording the behavior long enough to get a good measure of its average level. When you have enough information, define the average level of the behavior. On the average, the behavior occurs:

_____

Charting Behavior

You may find it helpful to create a visual picture of the level of a behavior by putting it on a graph. For example, the teacher described earlier who counted the number of times a day a student left his seat without permission made this graph:

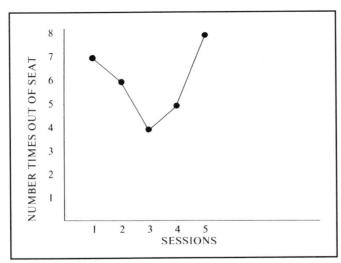

An employer's record of the number of coffee breaks taken by a secretary was graphed as follows:

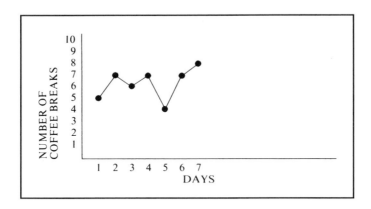

Charting Behavior Exercise (optional)

At the end of this text, before the References, is a sample Raw Data Sheet that many persons use to create a visual display of the target behavior. You may want to use that form to display the behavior you have chosen to change. The vertical axis shows the level of the behavior. Days or sessions go across the horizontal axis.

Chart the behavior you have measured by using a data point for each observation session. This record of the behavior before you try to change it is called a *baseline.* Ask your instructor to help you chart it if you are uncertain about how to do it. (Further discussion of measuring and charting behavior may be found in Hall & Van Houten, 1983.)

▶ **Step 4: Set a goal for the target behavior.**

Once you have measured the level of the behavior you wish to change, it is a good idea to set a goal. For example, the employer who was concerned about the number of coffee breaks his secretary took decided it would be sufficient improvement if she took no more than three per day.

Indicate here the target level of the behavior you have chosen: _____

_____

_____

_____

▶ **Step 5: Decide where the time-out place should be.**

Once the behavior you want to decrease has been defined and you have measured it to get an idea of its present level, you need to plan how you will go about using time-out. In selecting your procedure, there are a number of things to think about.

Although there are many ways time-out can be used, one of the most effective is to remove the person to a place that offers little opportunity to do or see anything that may be fun or rewarding. In the home, the bathroom is usually the best time-out room. There is little room to move around and it is usually much less interesting than the bedroom, family room, or kitchen. It is also possible to use the laundry room or bedroom from which access to TV, toys, or other playthings has been eliminated. In school, a workroom, a special booth, the principal's office, or the hallway can be used. In the classroom, a corner, a desk away from other children, or even the child's own desk if all work and play materials have been removed, can be a time-out place. In institutions, special booths, bedrooms, or therapy rooms are potential time-out areas. In sports or play activities, a player may be removed from the game or told to go to the corner of the playground. In the neighborhood play lot or in the backyard, the person can be told to leave the area. In business, a worker can be temporarily assigned to a less desirable job or to work in a less stimulating environment, or may be suspended from work altogether for a short time.

Any place selected should meet the following requirements:

1. It should be safe. For example, if the bathroom is used, all medication, razors, and other items that might cause harm to the child should be removed or put out of reach. Similar precautions should be taken in the laundry room or storage areas. A chair in a corner of a room or a hallway or a certain area on

the playground may be used for time-out if it is arranged so visitors and other children do not approach, talk to, or give other attention to the person in time-out. A child can also be put in time-out at his own task, work, or play area. If you are working alone with a child, you can remove play or work materials from his or her reach and turn away from him or her or leave the room. The true test of the place you choose is whether or not it decreases the behavior you have set out to change.

2. It should be free from toys, games, stereos, radios, or other things that might be interesting or provide enjoyment.

3. The place you choose should be well lighted and easily monitored. The child should not be afraid to go to the time-out place. It should not be dark or small enough to be frightening. You should also be able to monitor the child. This is especially important in a school or institution where you may have responsibility for other children. If you cannot monitor the child in time-out, you should arrange for an aide, the principal, or another adult to do so. This is one advantage of providing a time-out area within the classroom.

4. The place you choose should be arranged so you can put the person there with a minimum of time and effort and with as little distraction as possible. It should be a place the person can go in a few seconds with no more instruction than, "Go to time-out."

Selecting a Time-Out Place

With the conditions outlined above in mind, select a time-out place for the person whose behavior you plan to decrease.

Answer the following questions:

1. Name the time-out place. _____

2. Is it safe?   Yes ☐   No ☐   If not, what will you need to do to make it safe?

(continues)

3. Is it free of distractions that the person might find fun or interesting?
   Yes ☐   No ☐   If not, what can you do to make it less interesting?

   _____

   _____

4. Is it well lighted and familiar enough that the person will not be frightened when placed there?   Yes ☐   No ☐

5. Is it a place the person can get to quickly and with little distraction once you say, "Go to time-out"?   Yes ☐   No ☐

Check your responses with your instructor. If he or she agrees that the time-out place is a good one, you are ready to proceed.

▶ Step 6: Make sure the environment is rewarding.

Now that you have decided whose behavior you plan to change, what behavior you will decrease, and where the time-out place is, you are ready to plan how to implement the time-out procedure. First, however, you must make certain that the person is receiving reinforcement from you and the environment. To be effective, time-out must remove the person from toys, activities, materials, and positive attention from you and others. If the person is already being ignored and does not have access to interesting activities and materials in the environment before time-out, then time-out will not work.

With this in mind, list the reinforcers available to the person when he or she is not in time-out.

   _____

   _____

Are there some things you can do to make the environment more reinforcing?
Yes ☐   No ☐   If yes, what? _____

   _____

▶ Step 7: Decide how long time-out will last.

The next step in using time-out is to determine how long time-out will last. Most adults tend to make time-out last too long. If time-out is too long, it prevents the person from exhibiting or practicing the behavior you want, it makes it less likely you will use time-out every time the behavior occurs, and it can make having the person in time-out punishing to you. Short periods of time-out are more effective in decreasing behavior. Keep in mind that, to a child, 3 or 4 minutes on a chair or in the bathroom can be an eternity if there are things he or she wants to be doing elsewhere.

The time-out period should last from 2 to 5 minutes, and certainly no longer than 1 minute for each year of the person's age.

Indicate here how long a time-out period you plan to use. _____

A kitchen timer makes an excellent timekeeper for a time-out period. It is easy to set and provides a clear signal that time-out is over. It can also be reset if the person in time-out misbehaves.

Indicate here how you plan to keep track of time. _____

▶ Step 8: Practice by role-playing time-out.

After consulting with a psychologist, Dr. Jack Grinstead, because of their concern about their 4-year-old daughter, Janice, Paul and Dorothy Kennedy decided to use a time-out procedure to stop Janice from hitting her younger sister, Laura. They determined that Janice hit Laura about two or three times a day, and decided with Dr. Grinstead exactly how they would conduct time-out. Dr. Grinstead suggested that they practice role-playing time-out prior to implementing it with their daughter. First he set the scene. Then he took the role of one of the parents, and asked Dorothy Kennedy to play the role of Janice and Paul Kennedy to act as a recorder. On the recording sheet, Paul checked whether Dr. Grinstead remembered to carry out all the steps of the time-out procedure. Then they switched places. Mrs. Kennedy recorded, as Mr. Kennedy played himself and Dr. Grinstead played Janice. Finally, Mrs. Kennedy played herself, as Mr. Kennedy played Janice and Dr. Grinstead recorded.

The Scene:

Janice: Your parents have explained time-out to you and have even practiced it. However, you have decided to resist time-out to see if they really plan to carry it out.

Mr. or Mrs. Kennedy: You are determined to carry out the time-out procedure calmly and effectively. You will explain it, practice it, and then carry it out.

Recorder: This person guides the parents through all the steps and gives feedback on how well the person playing Janice's parent uses the time-out components listed on the recording sheet.

Mr. Kennedy recorded that Dr. Grinstead did a good job of carrying out the time-out procedures; however, he noted that Dr. Grinstead scolded Janice and also slipped when he said something to her when she was in time-out. It was not necessary for him to remove a backup privilege because Janice was not that resistant. When Mr. Kennedy role-played the parent, he did everything correctly except for ignoring one of Janice's objections. By the time it was her turn, Mrs. Kennedy was able to carry out time-out without any errors.

Set up your own role-playing situation. Just as with the Kennedys, it may be helpful for you to role-play your time-out procedure.

Your instructor, your spouse, your colleagues, or another person should help you set up a role-playing situation. You will need three persons, one to play you, one to play the person who will go to time-out, and one to record. Each should shift roles so that you go through the exercise three times, once for each position.

(continues)

Sample Recording Sheet: Role-Playing Time-Out

	Person Playing Parent		
Parent Behavior	**Dr. Grinstead**	**Mr. Kennedy**	**Mrs. Kennedy**
Practice			
1. Told Janice the rule for time-out (her behavior, what she must do, how long time-out would last) in simple language before using it	✔	✔	✔
2. Used a calm voice and positive language in the explanation	✔	✔	✔
3. Ignored all arguments and objections	✔	O	✔
4. Practiced the time-out procedure with Janice	✔	✔	✔
Time-Out			
1. Used time-out within 5 seconds the next time the behavior occurred	✔	✔	✔
2. Explained briefly why Janice was going to time-out	✔	✔	✔
3. Kept voice calm, did not scold	O	✔	✔
4. Ignored arguments and objections	✔	✔	✔
5. Began timing as soon as Janice entered time-out	✔	✔	✔
6. Did not give attention to Janice while in time-out	O	✔	✔
7. Added time in a calm voice if Janice left time-out or misbehaved	✔	✔	✔
8. Backed up time-out by removing TV privilege for the day if time-out went beyond 30 minutes	✔	✔	✔
9. Allowed Janice to leave it after time-out interval was over if Janice behaved	✔	✔	✔
10. Praised Janice for good behavior as soon as possible after time-out	✔	✔	✔

(continues)

Scene: Set the scene describing the following roles.

Target person: _____

_____

Your role: _____

_____

Recorder: Will guide the role-playing and give feedback.

Recording Sheet: Role-Playing Time-Out

	Person Playing Parent		
	1	**2**	**3**
Parent Behavior	_____	_____	_____
Practice			
1.			
2.			
3.			
4.			
Time-Out			
1.			
2.			
3.			
4.			
5.			
6.			
7.			
8.			
9.			
10.			

▶ **Step 9: Explain time-out to the person.**

There is one more preliminary step before beginning your time-out procedure. That step is to explain time-out and the rules for its use to the person on whom you intend to use it. This step will make it much easier for you to use time-out without showing emotion and it will help avoid verbal outbursts and tantrums when you begin using it. The following are things to remember in making your explanation.

1. Sit down with the person and explain that you love or care or are concerned about him or her and that is why you are going to begin a procedure that will help him or her to stop a behavior that has been causing a problem. Do this without nagging or scolding.

2. Explain the exact behavior that will result in time-out.

3. Explain that every time that behavior occurs, he or she will be put in time-out.

4. Tell how long time-out will last and how the person will know when it is over.

5. Explain that if he or she goes quietly and behaves, he or she can come out when the time is up. If he or she argues, leaves time-out, yells, or kicks the door, the time will be increased 1 minute for each outburst. If the person makes a mess, he or she must clean it up before leaving time-out. If the person breaks something, he or she will be expected to pay for it. If the extra time in time-out reaches more than 30 minutes, tell the person that an additional consequence will occur. This will be a backup consequence you will have decided upon.

6. Do not expect the person to be enthusiastic about your explanations.

7. If the person is a small child, practice the procedure to make sure that he or she understands where to go when time-out begins.

▶ **Step 10: Begin to use time-out.**

Now you are almost ready to begin using time-out. There are several important things to keep in mind:

1. Once you have explained time-out to the person, begin carrying it out the very next time the behavior occurs.

2. After that, use time-out every time the behavior occurs.

3. Start time-out as soon as you can, preferably just as the behavior begins. This will cause the behavior to decrease more rapidly and will tend to stop the behavior before it becomes a major incident.

4. When the behavior occurs, identify it. Tell the child in a normal voice, "That's arguing (interrupting, fighting). Go to time-out." If he or she does not respond to verbal directions, say, "No" or "Stop" and lead him or her to the time-out place (or if that is the backup procedure you have chosen, take away toys and materials and remove yourself from the situation).

5. You may say something like, "In 4 minutes you may come out," or "When the timer rings you may come back and play." Do not nag, scold, show anger, or give explanations.

6. Ignore all protests except to calmly say, "That will cost 1 more minute of time-out."

7. Ignore statements such as, "I don't care if I have to go to time-out" or "I like time-out!" Don't let such Brer Rabbit and the briar patch statements sway you. Notice only whether or not time-out causes the behavior to decrease.

8. If the child begins to do the task after you say, "Go to time-out," do not let him or her escape time-out. Have the child go to time-out and then come back to do the task.

9. Set the timer or look at your watch or clock as soon as the person enters time-out.

10. If the person misbehaves while in time-out, ignore it except to add more time to time-out. If the person is exceptionally resistant, use the backup consequence you have planned. (See the later section titled "Potential Problems and What To Do If Resistance Occurs.")

11. Be sure to release the person from time-out as soon as the time-out interval is over.

12. Make certain you reinforce the person frequently when he or she is not misbehaving between time-out episodes. This should be done frequently at first, but less often as time goes on and the behavior improves.

13. Make certain you use time-out only for the behavior you have selected. If necessary, use other consequences for other misbehaviors. Do not shift to another behavior until the first one you have selected is under control.

14. Remember that it is extremely important for you to remain calm and matter-of-fact when using time-out. If you become angry and emotional, you lose control of yourself and the child.

▶ **Step 11: Review.**

You are now ready to use time-out to decrease the behavior you have selected. Summarize the information from the first eight steps.

1. **Select a candidate for time-out.**

   Name the candidate(s) you have selected: _____

   _____

2. **Define or pinpoint the behavior.**

   Describe the behavior you will change.

   Who? _____

   What? _____

   Where? _____

   When? _____

3. **Measure the behavior.**

   Describe the current level of the behavior you have measured.

   _____

   _____

   _____

4. **Set a goal for the target behavior.**

   What is the target level of the behavior you have chosen? _____

   _____

5. **Select the place for time-out.**

   Describe where the time-out place will be. _____

   _____

   _____

   _____

(continues)

6. **Make sure the environment outside time-out is rewarding.**

   List here what you have done to make the environment more reinforcing.

   _____

   _____

   _____

7. **Decide how long time-out will last.**

   Describe how long time-out will last and how you will keep track of it.

   Time-out will last _____

   I will keep track of it with _____

8. **Go back to page 19 where you have listed the things to remember in carrying out time-out during the role-playing activity.**

   Is the list complete?   Yes ☐   No ☐   If not, add any items you want to keep in mind:

   _____

   _____

   _____

▶ **Step 12: Maintain good behavior.**

Time-out is a mild form of punishment that, if used correctly, will always result in a decrease in the target behavior. It is a procedure you can carry out systematically and consistently without resorting to anger and displays of emotion.

If used properly, the behavior will soon come under control because the person will realize that every time he or she engages in a certain behavior, time-out will occur and that, in time-out, reinforcers are no longer available. Very soon you will find that you have to use time-out less and less often.

An important thing to remember is that the behavior may return if you forget to provide attention, praise, and other rewards for the kind of behavior you want in place of the old behavior. For a more complete presentation of how to reinforce the person with attention and praise, we suggest you look at *How To Use Systematic Attention and Approval* (Hall & Hall, 1998).

Once the behavior is eliminated and you have another problem behavior you can pinpoint, it is quite acceptable to use time-out on this second behavior. Do not try to use time-out for more than one or two behaviors at a time, and be sure to make it clear to the person what behavior will result in time-out. If you use time-out for too many behaviors at once, the person is liable to spend so much time in time-out that time-out will become ineffective.

Potential Problems and What To Do If Resistance Occurs

Although time-out appears easy, it can be very difficult if resistance occurs. You should be prepared and know what you are going to do if resistance occurs. A great deal of resistance can be prevented by calmly explaining the time-out procedure during a period of good behavior prior to using time-out.

Even so, resistance sometimes occurs. If the person has well-established habits of willfulness, it may take considerable time and effort for you to establish the time-out procedure. The following paragraphs should help you determine how to respond to difficulties faced in implementing time-out.

1. Be prepared to add time to time-out for refusing to go to time-out, as well as for yelling, screaming, kicking the door, turning over furniture, or swearing. If these things happen, be prepared to say, "That will cost 1 minute" or "that's 1 more minute." Keep your voice calm! If you raise your voice or scold, you are losing.

2. If a small child fails to go to time-out, it is appropriate to prompt the behavior by gently but firmly taking him or her by the arm and leading him or her to time-out. This should be done without explanation or comment except for the initial statement, "That's (name of undesired behavior). Go to time-out."

3. If the person makes a mess, he or she must clean it up before returning from time-out. Again, keep your voice calm as you insist the mess be cleaned up.

4. If the person breaks something, he or she should be required to pay for it. It can be deducted from an allowance or arrangements can be made for him or her to work it off.

5. If the person refuses to go to or behave in time-out and is assessed extra minutes up to a given amount (usually 30 minutes total), a backup consequence should be used. If the person resists going to or leaves time-out, it is easy to lead him or her back to the time-out place by placing the palm of one hand on the small of the person's back and pushing slightly, marching him or her to the time-out area. Even a large person will find it difficult to resist if this procedure is used. For young children, some authorities once advocated a sharp spank on the bottom administered without comment every time the child got off a time-out chair or left the time-out bathroom. Because one goal of using time-out is to avoid physically abusing the person,

it is better to take away a privilege or impose another negative consequence that costs the person more than going quietly to time-out. For example, a parent could tell a 10-year-old boy that if he accumulates 30 minutes of time-out he will lose the use of his bicycle, and if he continues to protest, additional days can be added to the loss of bicycle use. A student who protests or misbehaves when placed in time-out in the classroom can be sent to the principal's office for 30 minutes if prearrangements have been made for no one there to talk to or look at him or her (see Broden, Hall, Dunlap, & Clark, 1970). Other backups might include loss of TV for a day, loss of recess or recreation period, or anything that will be more costly in the eyes of the person than going to time-out for a few minutes. In business, if a person objects to reassignment to a less preferred job or work location for an hour, a half-day, or one shift, suspension without pay may be used as a backup. It is important that the backup procedure is spelled out clearly in advance, that such procedures are uniformly applied, and that there is no management or union opposition to such procedures. Remember that whatever the backup, it should be decided in advance, and the person should know it will occur if he or she does not cooperate. This will help you provide the backup consequence calmly and without emotion. Remember, if you raise your voice and speak in anger, you will be losing.

6. If the person tells you that you have no right to put him or her in time-out or to take away backup privileges, say, "Yes, I do," and add a minute to time-out or add a day to the loss of privilege and walk away. Do not argue.

7. If the behavior of concern (such as fighting or arguing) involves two persons, do not get trapped into deciding who started it or who is at fault. Place both in time-out. For example, at home, send one child to the bathroom and one to the utility room. In a business or industrial setting, it may be possible to assign the person to work in a warehouse or loading dock or some place where the tasks are more difficult and there is less opportunity for social contact.

8. If you find that in spite of your best intentions you are becoming angry, it is best to walk away. After you have calmed down, come back and begin by adding minutes to time-out or by taking away a privilege.

9. If the person is your child and exhibits the behavior in public, tell the child to stop and that he or she will have to go into time-out as soon as you get home. If he or she does not stop, it is best to take him or her home right then for time-out. Return to the public place later and repeat taking him or her to time-out as many times as necessary.

10. Some parents have successfully placed children in time-out in a public place, such as a store, by having them sit or stand with their faces toward a wall for a brief time-out period. This avoids having to leave the store and also avoids delaying time-out.

11. It may be necessary to guide some young children to the time-out place and stay with them for a while until they understand the procedure.

▶ **Step 13: Evaluate the results.**

It is important to continue observing the behavior you measured to see if time-out made a change. Be prepared to record results of your efforts during the first week you try time-out.

Days or Sessions	1	2	3	4	5	6	7
Level of Behavior							

How does this level compare with the average level before you began?

_____

An increase? ☐   A decrease? ☐   No change? ☐

How did the person respond? _____

_____

_____

_____

Did the behavior get worse at first?   Yes ☐   No ☐

When did you first notice an improvement in the behavior? _____

_____

_____

_____

_____

Were you able to carry out time-out without showing anger?   Yes ☐   No ☐

Did you have to use a backup consequence?   Yes ☐   No ☐
If yes, how many times? _____

(continues)

Are you comfortable enough with time-out that you could use it for another behavior if it becomes necessary?   Yes ☐   No ☐   If you have another behavior you think you will decrease with time-out, what is it?

_____

_____

_____

_____

Who? _____

What? _____

Where? _____

When? _____

Making a graph of a behavior provides a visual display of how the behavior has been affected. Below is a chart of tantrum behavior in a 7-year-old boy before and after time-out.

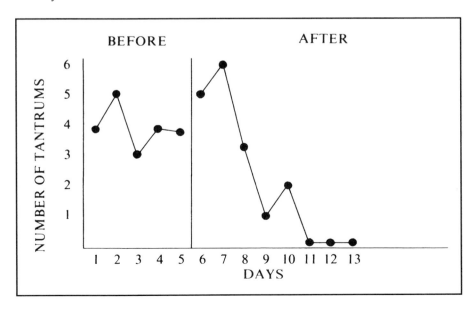

Charting Behavior (optional)

Using the Raw Data Sheet provided, make a record of the behavior you are changing using time-out. If you have already charted the behavior (before you tried to change it), you have a baseline. Draw a vertical line to show where the baseline record ends, just as was done in the example. Now chart the behavior to show the level each day or each session after you began the time-out procedures. This will give you a visual comparison so that it will be easy to see how much the behavior changes after baseline.

Where To From Here?

This book has explained how to use time-out to decrease behavior of other persons whose behavior is out of control.

The examples used were simple and straightforward. They were chosen to be representative of a variety of behaviors that can be managed with time-out. The potential list of behaviors that lend themselves to time-out is almost unlimited; however, once you get a few key behaviors under control, it is unlikely that you will need to resort to time-out very often. This is especially true if you make sure you are providing plenty of attention and reinforcement for the behaviors you do want. A person cannot be misbehaving and behaving at the same time.

Keep in mind that time-out is not a trick. It is a procedure based on laws of behavior, and if properly applied it will always be effective. Parents, teachers, attendants, and others who use time-out appropriately will find that they need to resort to it less and less with any given person. Remember that if a person is spending too much time in time-out, you are probably not providing enough rewards for engaging in desirable behavior. Furthermore, a person who spends a lot of time in time-out is probably not learning very much.

As you use time-out, you should begin to see that behavior is quite lawful. Children and adults can be taught good behavior or bad. Time-out is one basic procedure for stopping behavior that is out of control without resorting to threats, anger, scolding, reprimands, terminating employment, spanking, and other methods that are frequently ineffective, unpleasant, or abusive.

Program Follow-up

This section should be reviewed and filled out 2 weeks after you have initiated your program. It will provide feedback to your instructor on how well time-out has worked for you.

(continues)

1. Were you able to decrease the behavior you set out to change?
    Yes ☐   No ☐

2. What changes did you observe? _____

    _____

    _____

3. What problems did you encounter? _____

    _____

    _____

    Were you able to solve them? If so, how? _____

    _____

    _____

4. Briefly describe any other behaviors you will attempt to change. _____

    _____

    _____

5. Is time-out a skill you think you can now use effectively?
    Yes ☐   No ☐   Maybe ☐

6. Comments _____

    _____

    _____

    _____

    _____

    _____

    _____

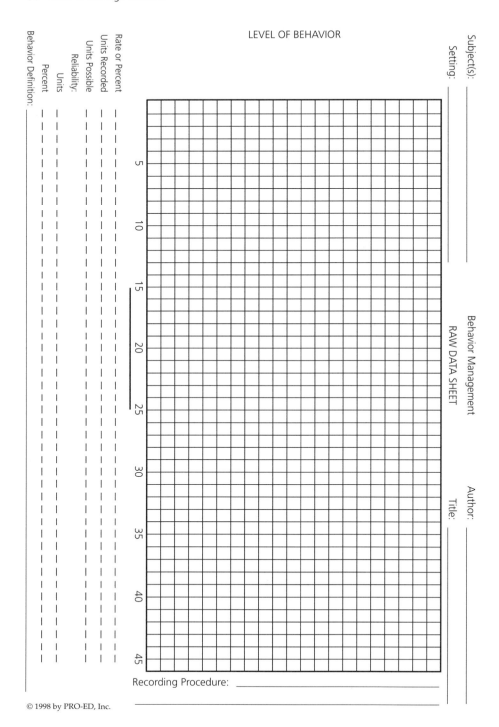

LEVEL OF BEHAVIOR

Subject(s): _____

Setting: _____

Behavior Management
RAW DATA SHEET

Author: _____

Title: _____

Rate or Percent
Units Recorded
Units Possible
Reliability:
    Units
    Percent
Behavior Definition:

Recording Procedure: _____

References and Further Reading

Axelrod, S. (1983). *Behavior modification for the classroom teacher.* New York: McGraw-Hill.

Broden, M., Hall, R. V., Dunlap, A., & Clark, R. (1970). Effects of teacher attention and a token reinforcement system in a junior high school special education class. *Exceptional Children, 36,* 341–349.

Brown, L., Nesbitt, J., Purvis, G., & Cossairt, A. (1978). The control of severe tantrum behavior through the use of a one-minute time-out procedure. In R. V. Hall & R. G. Fox, (Eds.), *Instructor's Manual for Responsive Teaching-Parenting Model Transparency Kit.* Lawrence, KS: H & H Enterprises.

Clark, H. B., Rowbury, R., Baer, A. M., & Baer, D. M. (1973). Time out as a punishing stimulus in continuous and intermittent schedules. *Journal of Applied Behavior Analysis, 6,* 443–455.

Craighead, W. E., Kazdin, A. E., & Mahoney, M. J. (1981). *Behavior modification: Principles, issues and applications.* Boston: Houghton Mifflin.

Flanagan, S., Adams, H. E., & Forehand, R. (1979). A comparison of four instructional techniques for teaching parents the use of time out. *Behavior Therapy, 10,* 94–100.

Gardner, H. L., Forehand, R., & Roberts, M. (1976). Time-out with children: Effects of an explanation and brief parent training on child and parent behaviors. *Journal of Abnormal Child Psychology, 4,* 277–287.

Hall, R. V., & Van Houten, R. (1983). *Managing behavior: Part 1. The measurement of behavior.* Austin, TX: PRO-ED.

Hall, R. V. (1975). *Managing behavior: Part 2. Basic principles.* Austin, TX: PRO-ED.

Hall, R. V., Fox, R., Willard, D., Goldsmith, L., Emerson, M., Owen, M., Davis, F., & Porcia, E. (1971). The teacher as observer and experimenter in the modification of disputing and talking-out behaviors. *Journal of Applied Behavior Analysis, 4,* 141–149.

Hall, R. V., & Hall, M. L., (1998). *How to use systematic attention and approval.* Austin, TX: PRO-ED.

Hall, R. V., Lund, D., & Jackson, D. (1968). Effects of teacher attention on study behavior. *Journal of Applied Behavior Analysis, 1,* 1–12.

Hobbs, S. A., & Forehand, R. (1975a). Differential effects of contingent and non-contingent release from time out on non-compliance and disruptive behavior of children. *Journal of Behavior Therapy and Experimental Psychiatry, 6,* 256–257.

Hobbs, S. A., & Forehand, R. (1975b). Effects of differential release from time out on children's deviant behavior. *Journal of Behavior Therapy and Experimental Psychiatry, 6,* 256–257.

Hobbs, S. A., & Forehand, R. (1977). Important parameters in the use of time out with children: A reexamination. *Journal of Behavior Therapy and Experimental Psychiatry, 3,* 365–370.

Hobbs, S. A., Forehand, R., & Murray, R. G. (1978). Effects of various durations of time out on the non-compliant behavior of children. *Behavior Therapy, 9,* 652–656.

Kazdin, A. E. (1994). *Behavior modification in applied settings.* Pacific Grove, CA: Brooks/Cole.

Lahey, B. B., McNees, M. P., & McNees, M. C. (1973). Control of an obscene "verbal tic" through time out in an elementary school classroom. *Journal of Applied Behavior Analysis, 6,* 101–104.

MacDonough, T. S., & Forehand, R. (1973). Response contingent time out: Important parameters in behavior modification with children. *Journal of Behavior Therapy and Experimental Psychiatry, 4,* 214–216.

Olson, R. L., & Roberts, M. W. (1987). Alternative treatments for sibling aggression. *Behavior Therapy, 18,* 243–250.

Roberts, M. W., Hatzenbueler, L. C., & Bean, A. W. (1981). The effects of differential attention and time out on child non-compliance. *Behavior Therapy, 12,* 93–99.

Rusch, F. R., Rose, T., & Greenwood, C. R. (1988). *Behavior analysis in special education.* Englewood Cliffs, NJ: Prentice-Hall.

Scarboro, M., E. & Forehand, R. (1975). Effects of two types of response contingent time out on compliance and oppositional behavior of children. *Journal of Experimental Child Psychology, 19,* 252–264.

Spitalnik, R., & Drabman, R. (1976). A classroom time out procedure for retarded children. *Journal of Behavior Therapy and Experimental Psychiatry, 7,* 17–21.

Sulzer-Azeroff, B., & Mayer, G. R. (1991). *Behavior analysis for lasting change.* Fort Worth, TX: Holt, Rinehart and Winston.

Wolf, M., Risley, T., & Mees, H. (1964). Application of operant conditioning procedures to the behavior problems of an autistic child. *Behavior Research and Therapy, 1,* 305–312.

Zeilberger, J., Sampen, S., & Sloane, H., Jr. (1968). Modification of a child's problem behaviors in the home with the mother as the therapist. *Journal of Applied Behavior Analysis, 1,* 47–53.

Notes

Notes